Photography for TEENS

8/12

Taking the Shot

Photography   Volume.   2

by Jason Skog

Content Consultant:
Kevin Jeffrey
Professional Photographer

COMPASS POINT BOOKS
a capstone imprint

Compass Point Books
1710 Roe Crest Drive
North Mankato, MN 56003

Editor: Jill Kalz
Designer: Ashlee Suker
Media Researcher: Svetlana Zhurkin
Production Specialist: Danielle Ceminsky

This book was manufactured with paper containing
at least 10 percent post-consumer waste.

Library of Congress Cataloging-in-Publication Data
Cataloging-in-publication information is on file with the Library of Congress.
ISBN 978-0-7565-4490-4 (library binding)
ISBN 978-0-7565-4533-8 (paperback)

Image Credits:
Capstone Studio: Karon Dubke, cover, 26, 27, 28, 29, 32 (top and middle); Corbis: Science
Faction/Steven Kazlowski, 36; Dreamstime: Eprom, 8, Ian Wilson, 14, Julija Sapic, 17
(top), Valentino2, 17 (bottom); iStockphoto: Mark Swallow, 35, Olga A. Lisitskaya, 37
(bottom); Jill Kalz, back cover (top), 19 (top), 20, 21 (bottom), 22 (top), 23, 24, 32
(bottom); Shutterstock: aggressor (pencil scribble), throughout, Alexandru Axon, 4, Anna
Jurkovska, 16 (top), Chuck Rausin, 42 (top), Emin Kuliyev, 40 (top), ExaMedia Photography,
18, George.M., 42 (bottom), Gilmanshin, 21 (top), govicinity, 19 (bottom), Gustavo Miguel
Fernandes, 39, Hu Xiao Fang, 11 (top), Igor Terekhov, 43, Ilja Masik, 22 (bottom), Kletr, 11
(bottom), 33, Konstantin Sutyagin, 17 (middle), Mircea Bezergheanu, 6, monalisha (dotted
circle), throughout, Nagy Melinda, 9 (bottom), Nejron Photo, 41, ntwowe, 1 (middle), 31
(bottom), Oleksii Nykonchuk, 15, OPIS, 30, 31 (top), Péter Gudella, 5, Ronen, back cover
(bottom), 13, Ryger (background texture), throughout, sint, 44, Stas Volik, 40 (bottom),
stavklem, 38, Tatjana Brila, 9 (top), Triff, 16 (bottom), Vatikaki, 7, VR Photos, 37 (top),
William Perugini, 34, Yen Hung Lin, back cover (middle), 25

Printed in the United States of America in Stevens Point, Wisconsin.
102011   006404WZS12

Table of Contents

Introduction

You've picked your subject. Framed it. Found the best light.

Now is the moment. THE moment. Time to take the shot. Time to turn your well-thought-out, carefully composed scene into one amazing photograph.

But wait.

Do you have the right tools to get the job done? More importantly, do you know how to use them? Taking good pictures requires a lot of practice and patience. But the more you know about your camera and what happens when you press the button, the better chance you have of capturing a moment and creating a lasting, memorable image. This book is filled with tips to help you get the most from your CLICK.

A photographer makes final preparations for taking a beautiful sunrise photo.

Chapter 1

Digital Camera Types and Uses

Self-portraits are a snap with a point-and-shoot digital camera.

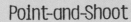

First things first: You can't take a photo if you don't have a camera. But with so many types of cameras out there, how do you choose? Let's look at the most common digital cameras and explore the best uses for each.

Point-and-Shoot

Point-and-shoot cameras are by far the most common, most affordable digital cameras in the market today. Size and simplicity are their biggest selling points. If you're just starting out, choose a point-and-shoot. These compact cameras are sleek, small, and almost entirely automated, with features such as auto-focus, auto-flash, and red-eye reduction. They do everything but take the picture for you.

Most point-and-shoot cameras are small enough to tuck in your shirt pocket. Others are slightly larger and more advanced, with more features, better lenses, and higher quality construction. Some include powerful zoom lenses and wide LCD screens on the back.

35mm Cameras

A 35mm camera is the standard for most professional photographers. Versatile, portable, and powerful, a 35mm camera takes its name from the width of the film that was used

A professional-level digital camera can be fitted with multiple lenses.

years ago. While digital 35mm cameras no longer use film, they're still called 35mm. Why? Because their style and features remain similar to earlier models.

A digital 35mm camera is also known as a D-SLR, a digital single-lens reflex camera. Interchangeable lenses are one of the strongest selling points for a D-SLR. But they also add to the camera's total price tag. D-SLRs can be outfitted with a countless variety of lenses, including long lenses for shooting distant objects and wide-angle lenses for panoramic views. They are the cameras used to create most of the photos you find in newspapers, magazines, and other media outlets.

A selection of interchangeable D-SLR lenses and a D-SLR camera body

CELL PHONE CAMERAS

If you have a cell phone, it probably has a camera in it. While cell phone cameras have limited power and features, and may not be a photographer's first choice, they are convenient. A cell phone's ability to quickly upload an image to the Internet or send it to friends makes these cameras a favorite. Spot a celebrity? See a tornado drop out of the sky? Catch your little brother dancing with the family dog? Click! Advances in technology ensure that image quality and other features of cell phone cameras will only get better in the months and years ahead.

Prosumer Cameras

In between the point-and-shoot cameras and the D-SLRs are the "prosumer" models. Prosumer is a combination of the words *professional* and *consumer*. Less expensive and lighter than some full-bodied D-SLR cameras, prosumer cameras offer much of the same performance of a D-SLR but without an interchangeable lens. On the flip side, because they're lighter and easier to handle, prosumer cameras are often not as rugged. Still, they represent a step up in image quality and versatility from point-and-shoot models. They give you the choice of using programmed settings or adjusting on your own. And they're great for taking photos in pretty much any situation.

An entry-level D-SLR with a standard lens and pop-up flash

Buying a Camera

Beware of buying a camera without holding it or trying it out. Some cameras are smaller than they look online or in an ad and can be tricky for a person with large hands to operate. Some cameras are loaded with features you may not need.

Get a feel for a camera's size and weight.

Visit a camera store and speak with a knowledgeable salesperson. Here's a checklist to keep you on track:

* Decide what you plan to use your camera for. Will you be taking spur-of-the-moment, candid pictures of friends? Carefully set-up nature shots? Sports photos?

* Hold the camera and see how it fits in your hand. How heavy is it, and how will you feel carrying it around? Remember, with D-SLRs you may have a number of extra lenses.

* Decide which features you need and which you can do without. Do you really need a waterproof camera for that one visit to the lake every two years?

* Take a few sample pictures. How sharp are they? How well does the flash work?

* Consider your budget. You'll also need a camera bag, memory cards, and batteries. It all adds up.

KNOW YOUR PARTS

To play a video game, you don't need to know what the various microchips inside a console look like or do. You don't even need to know what they're called. But you do need to understand how to use the controller. Same thing with a camera: You don't have to know *how* a camera takes a picture (although it wouldn't hurt), but you do need to know the key parts to operate it.

The most common parts are shown on the next page. See if you can identify them on your camera.

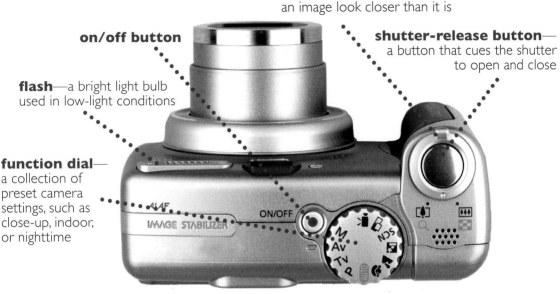

zoom—a function that makes an image look closer than it is

on/off button

shutter-release button— a button that cues the shutter to open and close

flash—a bright light bulb used in low-light conditions

function dial— a collection of preset camera settings, such as close-up, indoor, or nighttime

viewfinder—a small window through which to view a subject

lens—the glass "eye" of the camera

LCD screen—an electronic screen on which to preview or review photos

body—the main part of a camera

battery—a camera's power source; *note: the battery compartment for the camera shown is on the underside of the body*

memory card—a device used for data storage, including photos and video; SD cards are most common

MEGAPIXEL MADNESS

Manufacturers like to make a big deal about the number of megapixels their cameras have. Pixels are small squares or dots that are the smallest single element of a digital image that can be captured in a photograph. Mega means "million," so a camera with 3 megapixels has 3 million pixels. More megapixels mean more information and, therefore, more detail in an image.

But don't get caught up in the megapixel hype! A camera with a high megapixel rating doesn't automatically make it a fantastic camera. Megapixels are only one measure of a camera's performance. Unless you plan to blow up your image to mural size, a camera with 5 to 7 megapixels is usually enough, although cameras with 8 to 10 megapixels are increasingly becoming standard.

Be Ready for "the Moment"

Before you shoot, be ready to shoot. Sounds simple, right? So much of taking a great photograph depends on being in the right place at the right time. It also depends on the work you do and the knowledge you have before you take the picture.

Is your camera's battery charged? Is there enough room on the memory card? Is the lens clean? Take some test shots ahead of time to be sure things such as the flash and zoom are working smoothly. Also read and understand the owner's manual that came with your camera.

Being prepared makes capturing the moment easier.

2

Camera Settings, Set-up, and Handling

E very camera is different, so it's important to read and understand the owner's manual that comes with your camera. However, most cameras have several common features and settings, and there are basic handling practices that are good to know no matter what kind of camera you use. Check these out.

A slow shutter speed causes moving water to blur.

Shutter Speed

For point-and-shoot cameras, the shutter speed—the time the shutter stays open, allowing light to reach the image sensor—is set automatically. In bright light situations, the camera's shutter opens just a fraction of a second. In lower light the shutter remains open longer, letting in more light. D-SLRs allow you to control the shutter speed. Prosumer cameras give you the choice of using programmed settings or going solo.

Short exposure times are ideal for stopping motion and capturing quick movements, such as sports action. Long exposure times are needed for nighttime photos. The longer the shutter is open, the more prone the image is to blur. A tripod or other way of steadying the camera can come in handy.

A fast shutter speed can stop motion and capture individual water drops.

LIGHTING THE WAY

A camera's job is to capture light. No light, no photo.

Light enters the camera body through a curved piece of glass called a lens. It might help to think of the lens as the camera's eye. When you press the shutter-release button, a thin, lightweight shutter opens and closes (like an eyelid) according to the exposure time that either you or your automatic camera set. Light then travels through the aperture, hits a sensor (or film, if using a film camera), and an image is captured.

Aperture

Not only is incoming light controlled by the shutter, it's also managed by the aperture, which is kind of like the iris in your eye. The aperture is the hole at the back of a lens through which light passes before reaching the image sensor. It's a series of metal blades arranged in a circle that can be opened wide or narrowed to a small hole.

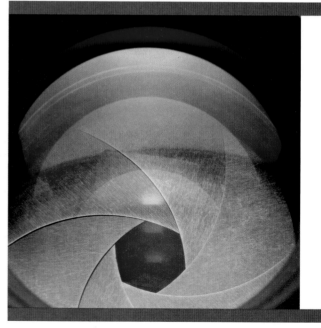

The aperture, open slightly

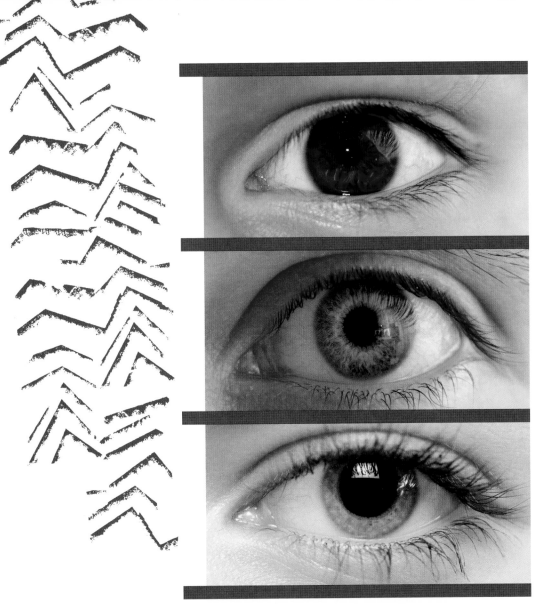

Like the aperture in an automatic camera, a pupil narrows in bright conditions and widens in dim conditions to let in the most light.

Both shutter speed and aperture control the light that reaches a camera's sensor or film. Automatic cameras open and close the aperture as needed. Manual cameras, on the other hand, let you adjust it yourself. Aperture is measured in f-stops. A low number, such as f/2, means a bigger aperture opening, with more light being allowed in. A high number means a smaller opening, with less light.

Aperture also affects the depth of field of a photographic image—what's in focus and what's not. An f-stop with a higher number (and smaller aperture) will generally lead to a longer focal length, meaning more objects at a distance will remain in focus. An f-stop with a lower number (and larger aperture) will generally mean a shallow depth of field. Close objects are in focus, and what lies beyond is blurry.

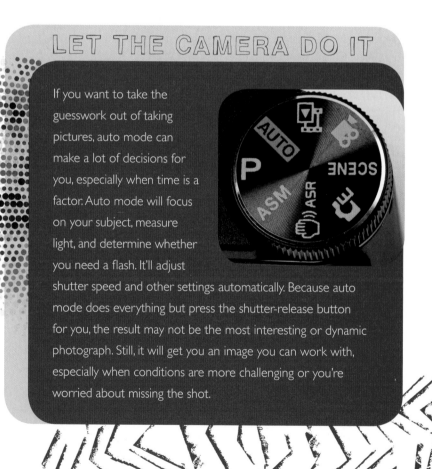

LET THE CAMERA DO IT

If you want to take the guesswork out of taking pictures, auto mode can make a lot of decisions for you, especially when time is a factor. Auto mode will focus on your subject, measure light, and determine whether you need a flash. It'll adjust shutter speed and other settings automatically. Because auto mode does everything but press the shutter-release button for you, the result may not be the most interesting or dynamic photograph. Still, it will get you an image you can work with, especially when conditions are more challenging or you're worried about missing the shot.

Distant objects remain in focus with a high f-stop number.

Near objects are in focus with a low f-stop number, while distant objects blur.

Special Modes

You're on a beach. Or at a football stadium. Or inside your favorite pizza place. If you want to take a picture, many of today's digital cameras have shooting modes specifically designed for those situations. Manufacturers program the camera's shutter speed, aperture, color tones, and flash to produce the best possible results for each situation. Special modes may include close-up, fireworks, museum, beach/snow, sports/action, party/indoor, dusk/dawn, sunset, or nighttime.

Flowers and bugs are popular close-up mode subjects.

Use a tripod or other steady surface with the fireworks mode.

Museum mode is perfect for places where flash photography isn't allowed.

Which special modes does your camera have? Play with them, and see how they compare to the auto setting.

Beach/Snow mode tones down light reflections off sand or snow.

Stopping motion is what sports/action mode does best.

STEP 1

Go outside just before sunset. Find the function dial on your camera and turn it to auto mode. Choose a subject and take a picture. Note the colors and shadows.

STEP 2

Next turn the function dial to sunset. (Some cameras have a scene stop on the dial that will take you to sunset mode.) Shoot the same subject. How has the image changed? How is the camera adjusting to the light conditions?

continued on next page

STEP 3

Finally switch to dusk/dawn mode and reshoot your subject. Which one of the three shots best mirrors reality? Which one do you like best?

STEP 4

Repeat this exercise with a different subject. Then move indoors and shoot one subject three times using the auto, party/indoor, and museum settings (if applicable).

Timers

Ever gone out with a group of friends and no one wants to take the picture because everyone wants to be in it? Even the most basic camera is likely to have a timer setting. It allows the camera to take the picture itself without you holding it and pressing the shutter-release button. Some timers let you set the number of seconds before the camera snaps the picture. Consider the amount of time you'll need to get from setting up the shot behind the camera to in front of the lens.

Timers are also helpful in situations that require longer exposures—during nighttime photography, for example. They can eliminate the movement created by you pressing the shutter-release button, which, though slight, may blur the image. Try mounting the camera on a tripod and setting the timer to take the picture for you, hands-free.

Setting a camera's timer allows for hands-free shooting.

STEP 1

Get two friends together. Mount your camera on a tripod or find a flat, level surface on which to set it.

STEP 2

Frame your friends in the shot. Leave space for yourself, and make sure your path from the camera to your friends is clear.

STEP 3

Set the timer. If you're given a choice between two lengths of time, choose the longer one, especially if you're new to timer photography.

STEP 4

Press the shutter-release button and quickly join your friends. Most cameras will beep a warning before they take the shot. Smile!

Light Meter

You can't create a photograph without light. But too much light can be a problem too. Today's cameras have built-in light meters that will either adjust the settings for you or warn you if you're about to take a picture when the light is less than ideal. Some cameras can be set to give you a light meter reading in real time. Then you can make adjustments by changing your camera angle, adding or reducing light, or moving your subject.

This light meter reading shows the photo will be overexposed (+) if settings aren't adjusted.

Continuous Burst Mode

Bam-bam-bam! Much the way a machine gun shoots multiple bullets with a single pull of the trigger, a camera set on "burst" mode captures many frames of action per second. That speed gives the photographer a better chance of getting the right image at the right time. Many point-and-shoot cameras include a burst mode that will take two or three frames per second, usually without a flash. Some prosumer models and most D-SLRs have a burst mode too. Some are capable of shooting six or more frames per second.

Burst mode stops the motion of a cartwheel.

Black-and-White vs. Color Photos

Years ago photographers had to choose between black-and-white and color film. Today many digital cameras can easily toggle back and forth between the two formats. Some situations seem suited to the more formal tone a black-and-white photo can set. Maybe it's a nature scene with striking shadows and interesting light—the kind noted photographer Ansel Adams shot. Maybe a family portrait feels more timeless and honest in black and

Color can bring life and energy to a photograph.

Black-and-white photos can feel more historical and serious than color photos.

white. Pick a few subjects—your grandma, the interior of your local library, and a tree, for example—and shoot them first in color, then in black and white. Which subjects look better in black and white? What qualities do the black-and-white photos have that the color photos don't?

ZOOM IN

The zoom feature on a camera gives you a closer look at a distant object. Most digital cameras have an optical and a digital zoom. Optical zoom refers to the camera's lens itself. Digital zoom is an additional level of zooming based on the closest image that can be captured with a camera's lens.

the subject at a distance

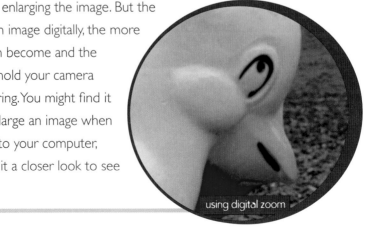
using optical zoom

An "x" indicates a camera's zoom power. A camera with a 10x zoom means you can magnify an object by a factor of 10. Let's say you have a camera with an optical zoom power of 10x. If an object is 60 feet away, your camera can zoom in so it appears only 6 feet away.

Digital zoom makes it seem as though your subject is even closer by enlarging the image. But the more you enlarge an image digitally, the more grainy the image can become and the harder it can be to hold your camera steady without blurring. You might find it easier to digitally enlarge an image when you download it onto your computer, where you can give it a closer look to see the effects.

using digital zoom

CAMERAS IN THE COMMUNITY

If you want to get the most out of your camera and learn a few tricks, enroll in a photography class at a local community college. Or sign up to be a member of an area photography club. Experienced photographers will help you learn more about your camera, show you how to care for it, and share pointers on how to get the shot you want.

IS FILM GONE FOREVER?

If you think film and film cameras are totally dead, think again. For many photographers, film is still the way to go, despite the added time and expense of purchasing and processing the film and making prints.

While advances in technology have made digital images comparable to film in many ways, some photographers prefer the image quality they get from film. Many film cameras can yield photos with considerably higher resolution than can be obtained with digital cameras. The tiny silver particles on film are randomly arranged. When they're exposed to light, they create a more uniform image that isn't subject to some of the limitations of digital. However, those differences aren't usually noticeable to the untrained eye unless the image is greatly enlarged.

Chapter 3

Extra Equipment and Accessories

The camera itself is only the beginning. Now come the extras! Some, such as memory cards and carrying cases, are essential. Others, such as fish-eye lenses, are special treats. Here are a few examples of additional equipment and accessories, their uses, and how they can improve your photos.

A fish-eye lens turns an ordinary train car into a funky art shot.

Memory Cards

Digital cameras store images on a small card called a memory card. There are several kinds, but the most common is SD (secure digital). An SD card uses flash memory, meaning there are no moving parts and the card can be filled, deleted, and reused over and over again. Memory cards have dropped in

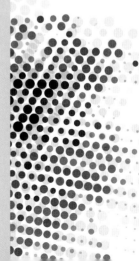

price dramatically since they were first introduced, even as their storage capacity has grown from a few megabytes to upward of 64 gigabytes. The larger capacity allows photographers to shoot high-resolution photographs and record video without worrying about running out of space.

An SD card is the most common type of memory card for digital cameras.

Tripods

If you're planning to take pictures that go beyond the candid, spur-of-the-moment shots of friends, consider buying a tripod. Necessary for nighttime and close-up photography, and useful in a variety of other situations, a tripod is a three-legged stand that holds a camera steady. A small bolt on its mounting platform screws into a threaded hole in the camera bottom. Most cameras today have this hole, called a tripod socket.

Think about where you're going to use your tripod most often. Out in the woods for nature shots? Try a lightweight tripod with flexible joints that allows you to set up just about anywhere for the coolest photos: on uneven rock, in a tree, or wrapped around a fence post. If you'll be shooting on level ground most of the time or indoors, an extendable-leg carbon fiber tripod may be your best bet.

A curious polar bear checks out an extendable-leg tripod.

Exposure Meters

Casual photographers usually use the trial-and-error method when it comes to lighting: Take a picture, review it, adjust the lighting, if necessary, and then keep taking pictures until the image looks just right. If your camera doesn't have a built-in light meter, a portable exposure meter is a precise method for checking lighting. It measures the light and indicates the correct settings for your camera or tells you to add a flash or other light source.

A hand-held exposure meter

LENS FILTERS

For cameras with interchangeable lenses, lens filters can provide protection for the lens and create a variety of effects. Filters fit on the end of a lens. They're threaded so they can be screwed into place by hand. Some filters absorb ultraviolet rays, reducing glare and haze in a photograph. Others reduce certain colors, such as the blues that can dominate some outdoor photographs. Some filters can even create starbursts or small rainbows of color, or wash the image in a sepia tone for an old-fashioned feel.

Lenses

If you have a D-SLR camera, you have the option of swapping out lenses. Most D-SLRs come with a standard 35mm lens that is just right for most daily photography needs. But if you want to branch out and try something new, here are a few of the most popular kinds of lenses.

Longer lenses allow photographers to take close, focused shots from a distance.

ZOOM A zoom lens is extremely versatile. It can give you a wider angle to capture more of a scene or zoom in to get closer to a subject far away.

telephoto This long lens brings distant subjects closer into view. Want a tight shot of the quarterback on the field or your favorite singer onstage but you're sitting back in the boonies? Get a telephoto.

Take first-row shots from the balcony with a telephoto lens.

wide-angle and fish-eye Both of these lenses capture wider scenes and provide a long depth of field, which means objects close up and far away remain in focus. A fish-eye lens is rounded like the eye of a fish and produces a very wide, curved image that looks like a reflection in a convex mirror.

A fish-eye lens bends an image to make it appear rounded, like a fish's eye.

A wide-angle lens is standard for landscape and architecture photography.

macro To capture pollen grains on a bee's leg or a raindrop balanced on a flower petal, use a macro lens. Macro lenses let you get very close to a subject to reveal the smallest details.

A macro lens brings tiny details into focus.

Rigid Cases

For the most secure camera storage, foam-lined, hardshell cases with a waterproof and dust-proof seal are hard to beat. These rugged plastic or metal cases offer protection against the roughest baggage handlers or nasty weather conditions.

Rigid cases are typically used by professional photographers who travel often. But they're also a good choice for hobbyists who've spent a lot of money on equipment and don't want to risk damaging their investment.

PUT A HOOD ON THAT LENS

One of the most basic and affordable accessories for interchangeable lenses is a lens hood. It's a flared ring that goes over the end of a lens. A lens hood helps block out glare from the sun or any other unwanted light that can interfere with an image. You can test how it works by holding your hand above the end of your lens and blocking the glare or by making a temporary hood out of heavy black paper. Roll the paper into a cylinder or cone the same diameter as your lens and tape it so it reaches out a few inches past the end of your lens.

IT'S IN THE BAG

Common sense: If you're going to invest in something as expensive and relatively fragile as a camera, it makes sense to invest in something to protect it. A padded, water resistant camera case works well for basic point-and-shoot cameras. For more sophisticated cameras, look for a bag that's large enough to hold not only the camera, but also the lenses, extra batteries, and memory cards. It should be padded, water resistant, and well-crafted, with sturdy closures and straps.

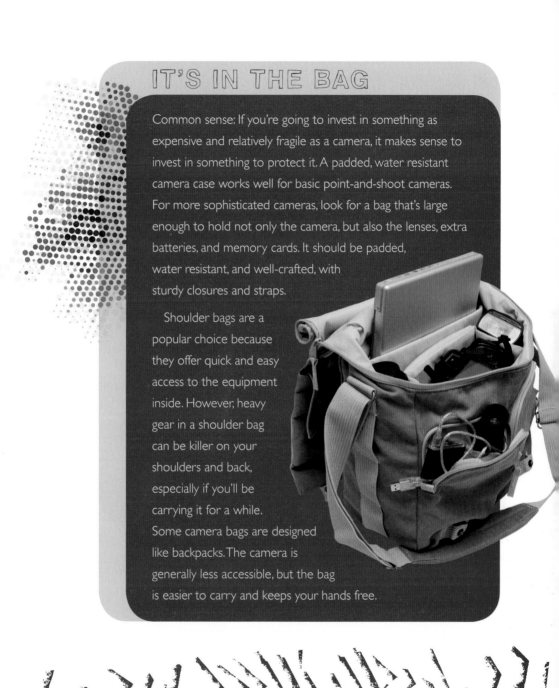

Shoulder bags are a popular choice because they offer quick and easy access to the equipment inside. However, heavy gear in a shoulder bag can be killer on your shoulders and back, especially if you'll be carrying it for a while. Some camera bags are designed like backpacks. The camera is generally less accessible, but the bag is easier to carry and keeps your hands free.

TIME TO SHOOT

Getting a great shot isn't about having the most expensive, most feature-heavy camera. It's not about buying every accessory under the sun. It's about understanding your equipment and knowing how to get the most out of it, no matter what kind of camera you have. Getting a great shot is about practice and not being afraid to play and make mistakes. It's about being ready.

Are you ready? Then go take that shot!

GLOSSARY

aperture–an opening in a photographic lens that lets in light

composition–the way pieces are put together to form a whole

flash–a bright light bulb that flashes for an instant to better light the subject of a photograph

lens–a piece of curved glass in a camera that can bend light and focus images

panorama–a wide view of an area

shutter–the part of a camera that allows light in

tripod–a stand with three legs

versatile–useful in many ways

viewfinder–a small window through which the subject of a photograph can be viewed

FURTHER READING

Ang, Tom. *Digital Photography: An Introduction.* New York: DK Pub., 2010.

Campbell, Marc, and Dave Long. *Digital Photography for Teens.* Boston: Thomson Course Technology, 2007.

Johnson, Dave. *How to Do Everything: Digital Camera.* New York: McGraw-Hill, 2008.

McNally, Joe. *The Moment It Clicks: Photography Secrets from One of the World's Top Shooters.* Berkeley, Calif.: New Riders, 2008.

ON THE WEB

Use FactHound to find Internet sites related to this book. All of the sites on FactHound have been researched by our staff.

Here's all you do:

Visit *www.facthound.com*

Type in this code: 9780756544904

ABOUT THE AUTHOR

Jason Skog has written several books for young readers. He is a freelance writer and former newspaper reporter living in Brooklyn, New York, with his wife and two young sons.

SELECT BIBLIOGRAPHY

Ang, Tom. *Digital Photographer's Handbook.* New York: Dorling Kindersley, 2008.

Busch, David D. *Digital SLR Cameras & Photography for Dummies.* Indianapolis: Wiley Pub., 2009.

Kelby, Scott. *The Digital Photography Book, Volume 3, the Step-by-Step Secrets for How to Make Your Photos Look Like the Pros'!* Berkeley, Calif.: Peachpit Press, 2010.

Wignall, Jeff. *Focus on Digital Photography Basics.* Focus On series. New York: Lark Books, 2010.

Look for all the books in the Photography for TEENS series:

INDEX